VIRGINIA GAY is an actor, writer and director. She has written two plays, *Cyrano,* and *The Boomkak Panto* (Belvoir St Theatre), and is working on her third, *Mama Does Derby* (Windmill). In 2024, she won a Fringe First Award for Most Outstanding New Writing at the Edinburgh Fringe for her adaptation of *Cyrano*, and was named one of the Fringe Five – Edinburgh's Five Breakout Theatre Makers – by *The Stage*. The production went on to a five-star season at The Park Theatre, London. She won a Sydney Theatre Award for Best Actress in *Calamity Jane,* received a Logie nomination for Most Outstanding Actress in *After The Verdict,* and played an absolute nightmare human in Season Two of *Colin From Accounts*. She starred in the film *Judy & Punch* (also starring Mia Wasikowska) which premiered at Sundance, in *Savage River* for Aquarius Films (also starring Katherine Langford), and *Safe Home* for SBS (also starring Aisha Dee), and is thrilled to be the artistic director of the Adelaide Cabaret Festival 2024/25. She spent four years pretending to be a nurse on *All Saints*, and five years pretending to know a lot about high finance on *Winners & Losers*. That last one, particularly, was a stretch.

Tuuli Narkle as Roxanne and Virginia Gay as Cyrano in MTC's production of CYRANO*, 2022 (Photo: Jeff Busby)*

Holly Austin as 3, Claude Jabbour as Yan and Virginia Gay as Cyrano in MTC's production of CYRANO*, 2022 (Photo: Jeff Busby)*

VIRGINIA GAY

CYRANO

after

EDMOND ROSTAND

CURRENCY PRESS
The performing arts publisher

CURRENCY PLAYS

First published in 2025
by Currency Press Pty Ltd,
Gadigal Land, Suite 310, 46–56 Kippax Street, Surry Hills, NSW 2010, Australia
enquiries@currency.com.au
www.currency.com.au

Copyright: *'Flood the field with love': the queering of* Cyrano © Annabel Crabb, 2025; *Cyrano* © Virginia Gay, 2025.

COPYING FOR EDUCATIONAL PURPOSES

The Australian *Copyright Act 1968* [Act] allows a maximum of one chapter or 10% of this book, whichever is the greater, to be copied by any educational institution for its educational purposes provided that that educational institution [or the body that administers it] has given a remuneration notice to Copyright Agency [CA] under the Act.

For details of the CA licence for educational institutions contact CA, 12 / 66 Goulburn Street, Sydney, NSW, 2000; tel: within Australia 1800 066 844 toll free; outside Australia 61 2 9394 7600; fax: 61 2 9394 7601; email: memberservices@copyright.com.au

COPYING FOR OTHER PURPOSES

Except as permitted under the Act, for example a fair dealing for the purposes of study, research, criticism or review, no part of this book may be reproduced, stored in a retrieval system, or transmitted in any form or by any means without prior written permission. All enquiries should be made to the publisher at the address above.

Any performance or public reading of *Cyrano* is forbidden unless a licence has been received from the author or the author's agent. The purchase of this book in no way gives the purchaser the right to perform the play in public, whether by means of a staged production or a reading. All applications for public performance should be addressed to the author c / —LMCM, Lisa Mann Creative Management, PO Box 3145, Redfern NSW 2016; tel: +61 2 9387 8207; email: info@lmcm.com.au

Currency Press has made every reasonable effort to identify, and gain the permission of, the artists who appear in the photographs that illustrate this play.

Typeset by Brighton Gray for Currency Press.
Printed by Fineline Print + Copy Services, Revesby, NSW.
Cover design by Emma Vine for Currency Press.

Currency Press acknowledges the Traditional Owners of the Country on which we live and work. We pay our respects to all Aboriginal and Torres Strait Islander Elders, past and present.

A catalogue record for this book is available from the National Library of Australia

Contents

Cast in MTC's production of Cyrano*, 2022. From left to right on the top: Tuuli Narkle as Roxanne, Milo Hartill as 1, Holly Austin as 3. Bottom: Robin Goldsworthy as 2 and Claude Jabbour as Yan (Photo: Jeff Busby)*

Tuuli Narkle as Roxanne in MTC's production of Cyrano*, 2022 (Photo: Jeff Busby)*

‘Flood the field with love’: the queering of *Cyrano*

One of the big mistakes people make about writing is to think that it starts with the typing. Actually, great writing starts way, way, WAY earlier than that, before a single page is despoiled or a pixel sacrificed, before the writer has commenced the process of dispelling her absolute and queasy certainty that this is not going to work and she would be better off doing almost anything else. Before *that*, even.

In fact, I would go so far as to say that most pieces of writing are already either bad or good, or (most commonly, and worst of all) in-between, by the time the first draft of the first sentence comes plopping into the world.

Why?

Because the most important part of writing isn’t the writing. It’s the noticing. It’s the glimpsing of something in outline, a peripheral flicker of something that isn’t there yet but could be, one day. It’s the sensing of a pulse, a space, a sentiment as yet unexpressed, something sparkly that snags and nags behind the quotidian bustle of life and time. A possibility. A quickening—to borrow the lovely old word for when babies first move in the womb.

It’s the noticing.

Although Virginia Gay has a comedically vast range of familiarities (she is probably the only person I can think of who could feasibly be stopped in the street and asked, ‘Hey! Aren’t you that nurse from *All Saints*? No! You’re the singer. Way—WAIT, no, the *dancer*. No—UGH. Don’t tell me. You were on that book show, weren’t you? Hang on, were you a COP? On the telly?’ and have all of those things be true), the big thing about Virginia is that she is a noticer: a chronic noticer; a ribald noticer; a restless, twirling, epic, infectious, warm-hearted, WEAPONS-GRADE noticer.

While, technically, it might be true to say that this adaptation of *Cyrano* started when Virginia Gay began to type it, it’s closer to the mark to peg its beginnings to pre-pandemic London, when Virginia saw James McAvoy's *Cyrano* and, by interval, had irretrievably noticed the possibility that this familiar character might be begging to be female and queer. But even that's not quite right—because even though this is an adaptation of a famous play that in part was ignited by Virginia seeing McAvoy's play and noticing the faint outline of a new interpretation, the DNA strands with which Virginia's *Cyrano* are so fibrously and enjoyably strung come from half a lifetime of being an unusually tall and broad-shouldered woman in a waif-based industry, and of noticing how that works. By extension, she has spent half a lifetime noticing how other inclusions and exclusions work for other people around her.

This is a play unmistakeably powered by (to use the playwright's own words) 'a big, tall weirdo with a secret huge heart'.

Big, tall weirdos with secret huge hearts do it tough from time to time. But the advantages of being born a tiny bit outside the lines are multiple. You get very good at noticing things. And you're never too anxious about rewriting the story, seeing as it wasn't really written for you anyway.

In this *Cyrano*, Virginia hasn't bothered with the prosthetic nose. She's given everyone presents—boobs for Cyrano, a brain for Roxanne—and crisply despatched the customary ending in which everybody dies unhappily.

Instead, she's rewritten the play in a way that opens its arms to every single person in its orbit. The audience is involved from the first second. No character is obliged to slog on without a funny line; not even the crew.

'This is not fair!' complains Cyrano, when handsome Yan makes his spotlit entrance. 'Who's lighting this! I had to do mine in silence and a wash?' (To the audience: 'No, don't applaud him. You're better than that.')

On stage, Virginia's *Cyrano* is pumped full of life and love. A play about thwartedness and stoppered longing is somehow opened up and helium-lifted into something more universal and triumphant. It's a lot of fun.

But when you sit down in a quiet place to read the script, the writer's neat, intelligent stitches are nicely appreciable; Cyrano's famous self-deprecation is layered elegantly with the playwright's own wry acknowledgment of what she's done to the original.

CYRANO: why do we keep telling the old stories? … they end badly, for everyone.

YAN: I don't know, they usually work out all right for me.

CYRANO: even for you. in the old story, you go off to war. all of you. you don't come back.

In this *Cyrano*, brains win out over beauty. Nobody goes to war. Cyrano gets the girl.

And honestly, at this precise point in the parabola of human history, plagued as we are by conflict and nastiness and actual plagues, who among us is not ready for an hour or two of theatre in which the good end happily?

This may, in addition, be how the play manages to outrun all the awkwardness that the modern world bowls up for a *Cyrano* remake. Let's face it: in the twitchy league of 'Well-Loved Cultural Icons That Make You Feel A Bit Not Quite Right When You Take A Closer Look', *Cyrano* is right up there with 'Baby, It's Cold Outside'. Man with a prohibitively large honker? Gets the hots for his beautiful but vapid cousin? And … catfishes her? Paging the sensitivity reader to reception, immediately!

Virginia's answer to such awkward complexities turns out to be quite simple: Flood the field with love. Love for human beings in all their foolishness and confusion and self-loathing. The kind of love you can really swim around in, the kind that floods out when a secret huge heart cracks wide open.

And, in the end, why is a big nose even necessary to tell this old story? The nose was always an allegory, anyway—a beaky evocation of a much vaster human phenomenon, the crushing fear that one's weird, awkward, unlovable flesh is taking up or displacing space to which one is not quite entitled. That this space was designed for someone else. And it turns out the answer to this one is quite straightforward too. Make more space. Budge up. We can take more people in here. There's room. There really is.

Annabel Crabb

Tuuli Narke as Roxanne, Virginia Gay as Cyrano, Claude Jabbour as Yan, Robin Goldsworthy as 2, Holly Austin as 3 and Milo Hartill as 1 in MTC's production of CYRANO*, 2022 (Photo: Jeff Busby)*

Virginia Gay as Cyrano in MTC's production of CYRANO*, 2022 (Photo: Jeff Busby)*

Author's Note

Hi! Hello! Thank you so much for picking this up. Gosh, you look fab, don't you? Have you done something with your hair? Anyway, come, sit. Sit!

Why a female Cyrano? Great question! It always felt like a female story to me—'If only you thought a bit less, talked a bit less, and were a bit more conventionally attractive, things would be easier for you.' I feel like I've been told a version of that my whole life.

Why a queer Cyrano? A Queerano, if you will (and I won't, my producers talked me out of it, and honestly? Thank God). The central conceit, even in the original, reads as deeply queer—if I wasn't born in this body, if I'd been born into this *other* 'perfect' body, only then would I be the love interest for this brilliant person.

I saw the (utterly excellent) James McAvoy/Jamie Lloyd production of *Cyrano* just before a pandemic shut the world down. I bought two copies of the (utterly excellent) Martin Crimp adaptation at interval, thinking, 'I'll take this back to Melbourne Theatre Company and do it there' and went back in for the second half and had forgotten that EVERYBODY DIES. So French of them. But if you've got a queer, female Cyrano at the centre of it … Well, I don't want to be part of any storytelling that says queer love is impossible and you should 'bury your gays', so … what to do?

This play was written entirely in lockdown in LA, with a broken heart and an apoca-puppy by my side. Long, dark, empty nights stretching out before me, before us all—desperate for connection, but surviving on scraps. We could talk about the strange, sad half-birth of the first production of this show in Melbourne—shut down by a snap lockdown three hours before opening. We could talk about how an appearance on *Q+A* changed my life, and altered the course of the show's. How, when asked to do an excerpt from the show, I thought, 'I can't do the nose speech, even though it's the famous bit, because it's fuelled by self-hate, and we *cannot deal* with any more pain right now'. How I mangled the final scene (it's alright, I know the writer), delivered it down the lens, made you my scene partner (thanks, you were terrific), and I tried, as hard as I could, to let you know you weren't alone. Tried to reach all the big hearts in the little rooms in poor, cold, quiet Melbourne, and remind us of all the things we'd get up to again, soon, soon, soon. People get married to that text now, which is wild and beautiful and makes me feel a bit weird to write down, because I am Australian, and God forbid we should talk about something that makes our hearts glow.

But for the show to continue to live, it had to break free of the darkness, and the specificity, of its birth. There are different tragedies and travesties happening all over the world—the horrors continue, relentless, and seemingly unstoppable. Theatre, more than any art form, has the capacity to respond to where it is in the world right now, what's happening *right now*; the space we're in, the audience that we're speaking to. It's live. It lives. Each new cast and each new venue requires us to shape this show into something specifically for this moment. I cannot wait to see what future theatremakers make of this play.

Our *Cyrano* sometimes gets described as a love letter to hope and overcoming loneliness, but I think it is first and foremost a love letter to theatre—it's about the extraordinary act of making theatre. (And the original really does start in a theatre, I'm not making it up.) A person who keeps themselves separate from the action, but who writes these incredible scenes for other more attractive versions of themselves to play, is what it *feels* like to write a play—sitting alone in a room, moving characters about like chess pieces and doing terrible, wonderful things to them. It's powerful, to write those scenes, to have that control. But it's also isolating, and it's *fictional*. It's not the true business of living, the intimacy, the mess, the mistakes and struggle and work and (don't tell Cyrano) the surprising ease of loving and being loved (once you stop letting your trauma drive your narrative). Every rehearsal of every show starts with a blank stage, and we try to work out how to tell this story—we bicker and laugh and try to tip the balance toward our own ends to try and make something worthwhile. For you. We cannot make live theatre, especially not a comedy, without an audience. *You* are the final character.

In a tragedy, you can have perfect people who are crushed by external forces, but if you're writing a romantic comedy, you need to have imperfect people who learn and grow. So we leaned into the arrogance of Cyrano, the toxic masculinity of Yan, and the shallowness of Roxanne, then asked them to take off their armour. Like any good Greek chorus, our chorus are voices for the audience, but they're also amalgams of many characters in the original. No theatre company that values solvency is putting on a show with a cast of sixteen (please, in this economy??). The baker and the best friend got rolled into one; the antagonist and villain also became the tragedian; and then there's the little, fierce voice of the new. Naiveté is clownish and foolish, yes, but innocence is beautiful, and you need some shred of optimism to question the status quo, and say, 'it doesn't have to be like this'.

And as for Cyrano—where are the roles like this for women (and our trans and NB siblings)? Where are the roles that ask for such verbal dexterity, such physical agility, such wit, such fearlessness and such connection with a crowd? I wanted to write something for us, the big, tall weirdos with secret huge hearts. (You don't have to be tall to play this role, but the secret huge heart is non-negotiable.) And how can I re-write this story *as* a woman, when what happens at the heart of it, this 'grand romantic gesture', has a name now, and that name is 'catfishing'? I worked hard to make Roxanne Cyrano's equal in word and thought. Smarter, even, than Cyrano, with emotional intelligence as well as book-smarts—she knows what her body wants and she's not afraid to ask for it. We meet and fall in love with her at the same time as Cyrano. She's not a distantly desired object—she's real and flawed. She dazzles us with her wit and curiosity, which of course makes the betrayal so much more galling. And if there *is* betrayal at the heart of this classic romcom set up, then *why* are we still telling these old stories? What responsibility do we have to our audiences if we're mindlessly repeating and endorsing destructive behaviour? How do you *ever* try and jump the tracks of an old narrative, and reach for something more than the role you were given, more than what you thought you were worth?

I'd like to thank the cast of every production and every reading of this work. They have interrogated this play, poked and prodded it, thrown it up in the air with delight to see where bits land, and I could not love them more. Each one has brought so much of themselves to it—I am endlessly indebted. There is a special place in heaven for actors who deliver a line not only exactly as you heard it in your head, but better than you could ever possibly imagine. More truthful, more cutting, more breathtakingly funny. Who reveal discoveries and weave throughlines that enrich and strengthen the whole. What actors do is nothing short of literal magic and watching them breathe life into dust and ink will never cease to astonish me.

I am and always will be absurdly grateful to Michael and Bonnie from Roast for giving this show such an extraordinary second chance at life, on the other side of the world. I was raised on British comedies, on *Blackadder*, *The Norman Conquests*, *Fry and Laurie*, *Monty Python*, and *The Goodies*—I replayed VHS tapes, pored over transcripts, and obsessively re-read *Rosencrantz and Guildenstern are Dead.* It's absolutely wild to me to that this show had such a warm, loving season in the brisk, bright cold of a London winter. My tiny brain cannot deal with this.

A huge thanks to every creative who has touched every iteration of this show—thank you Sarah for fighting so hard for it and being such a part of its birth, thank you Gadsby, Xani, Paul, Kelly, Jo (and Bo!), Brett and Martina, and thanks to Virginia Trioli for not taking no for an answer. Thank you Clare, Amanda, Andy, Toby, Paul, Hannah and Naomi, our little UK family. Thank you to Alice and Leon and Gidget (the apoca-puppy!) for the pandemic sanctuary, and to my wonderful parents Pen and Rob, whose keen eye, love of rhythm, and willingness to talk about stories at any time of the day or night, taught me how to write.

I hope you enjoy reading the play. Hell, I hope you put it on. Send me some pics of it, if you do, and if you've got a question, or something happened in your production that you think I might love, or might make me scream with laughter, come find me on the internet. I'd love to hear about it.

I hope you go and flirt with someone you've always secretly adored. I hope you make wild, bold art, packed with ideas and heart and huge fucking laughs. I hope you take a big swing, even knowing you might miss. That's it. That's the whole thing. We hope. We try. We try again.

Love, V xx

Cyrano was first produced in 2022 by Melbourne Theatre Company, on the lands of the Boon Wurrung and Wurundjeri peoples of the Kulin Nation, directed by Sarah Goodes. The cast was as follows:

CYRANO	Virginia Gay
ROXANNE	Tuuli Narkle
YAN	Claude Jabbour
1	Milo Hartill
2	Robin Goldsworthy
3	Holly Austin

This production transferred to the Heath Ledger Theatre with Perth Festival/Black Swan in 2023, with Joel Jackson as YAN *and Zenya Carmellotti as* 1.

Cyrano had its European premiere in 2024 at Edinburgh Fringe Festival at The Traverse Theatre, directed by Clare Watson. The cast was as follows:

CYRANO	Virginia Gay
ROXANNE	Jessica Whitehurst
YAN	Brandon Grace
1	Tessa Wong
2	David Tarkenter
3	Tanvi Virmani

This production transferred to London's Park Theatre in late 2024, with Joseph Evans as YAN.

Script development on Cyrano *was aided by Australia Council for the Arts, Sydney Festival, City of Melbourne, Create NSW, and Roast Productions.*

CHARACTERS

CYRANO

ROXANNE

YAN

1

2

3

NOTES ON TEXT

words in (round brackets) are unspoken

a forward slash (/) indicates a point of interruption/overlapping dialogue

an ellipsis (…) suggests thinking and not necessarily rhythm

NOTES ON CASTING

as much diversity and inclusion as possible, please

ROXANNE is always from a BIPOC/global majority background

CYRANO is performed without 'a nose', and can be played by anybody who isn't male, white, straight, cis, and able-bodied

don't be cross, fellas—you have the rest of the canon. leave this for us xx

1.

an empty stage

2: [*portentous*] it starts in a theatre
1: yeah, we've done that bit
2: what? what bit?
1: the bit where it starts in a theatre
2: what do you mean?
1: we just did it. it starts in a theatre
2: what—just then? was that the beginning??
1: lights down, lights up, we have started, ergo, it starts in a theatre
2: 'ergo'

2 *is silenced with a look*

there's silence for a bit more as they stare at the space

big, isn't it?

everybody looks

1: so much air
2: but … heavy
1: heavy air. weird
2: the weight of expectation. [*sonorous voice*] the weight of history
1: are you gonna be like this the whole time?
2: maybe. [*losing courage*] I haven't decided yet. has it always been this big?
1: you mean, have we always felt so small?
2: I think I do
3: have you?

3 *has spoken for the first time*—1 *and* 2 *turn and look*

2: what?
3: always felt … so small?
2: well, not all the time. mostly I feel magnificent. just [*losing confidence*] not *right* now…
3: I have
1: what

3: small. felt it. always
1 / 2: … ah
3: I think
2: who's this?

1 *shakes her head*

3: I'm new. hullo!

1 *and* 2 *wave in a perfunctory fashion*

2: alright, so, assuming it starts in a theatre
1: which it does
3: and has
1: thank you
3: an empty theatre?
2: no, a full one
1: it starts with an audience waiting for a show to begin

1 *gestures to the audience. they are*

3: whoa
2: oh. right. well … then—
1: the balcony scene
2: straight away??
1: it's the famous bit, the bit that people remember
2: it starts with a fight
3: [*correcting*] it starts in a theatre
1 / 2: yeah, we've done that bit
3: oh
1: seduce 'em—with the balcony scene
2: oh god, why
1: it's all seduction, the whole thing's seduction
2: the whole show??
1: no, I mean life, it's all a seduction
2: life? life?? we're getting a bit big a bit soon, don't you think?
3: yeah
2: start with a fight
3: kick it off with a bang
2: kick it off literally
3: good, that's good

1: it's not good
2: everyone's a critic. we start with a fight so they see her win first, before the … you know
1: [*grim*] I do
3: what? what??
2: it doesn't end well
3: oh, really? I don't remember that
1: no one does. are we going with 'her'?
3: what?
2: 'him'?
3: oh. well. what do 'they' want?
2: I don't think this is *that* show
1: who are we to say what the show is—we're just the chorus
2: I have a fully developed character
3: me too
2: I have several fully developed characters
1: versatile
2: it starts in a theatre
1: oh my god
2: and then there's a fight
3: a fight!
2: and she wins
3: who's 'she'? which 'she'?
1: noble
2: quick-tempered
1: big-hearted
2: arrogant
1: merciless
2: the one with the …
1: DON'T SAY IT
2: it's important
3: don't say what?
2: the one with the
1: I mean it
3: mean what?
2: the one with the nose

a silence—they check to see if they've been overheard

3: a nose?
1: shhhhh
2: this thing …
3: ooo, is it big?
1: shhhhh!
2: huge
1: so huge
3: how huge?
1 / 2: SHHHHH!
1: and she's aware it's repellent
2: eats her up inside, you can see it
3: oooo, how terrible
1: oh christ, don't pity her
2: fuck no
1: she can't stand pity
3: I didn't … I wouldn't …
1: she'd destroy you if she heard
3: is she a fighter?
1 / 2: the best
1: slice you into a thousand pieces
2: flay you
1: ooo, she would, she'd flay you
3: I didn't do anything!
1: we're just letting you know
2: helping

a pause

I'm a bit disappointed by the…

2 *gestures to the costumes*

shouldn't there be ruffs?
1: ruffs?
2: and britches?
1: *should* there be?
3: is there music, at least?
1: music?
2: music!
1: oh, there's definitely music

whole cast forms a little troupe and makes some music

3: what's it about
2: what?
3: this whole thing. what's it about?
1 / 2: ahh
1: longing. I think
3: longing?
1: and isolation
2: and risk management
1: fucking hell
3: and this person with the [*gestures*]
1 / 2: shhhh
3: I didn't say anything!
2: you [*gestures*]—it's enough
3: central character?
1: without question
2: I think it's more of an ensemble piece
1: yeah, you would
2: she's self-destructive
1: most geniuses are
2: settle down
3: genii—

1 *and* 2 *glare at* 3

1: smartest person in the room
3: gotta feel good
2: gotta feel lonely
CYRANO: it does

2.

CYRANO *has appeared*

3: is this
2: yup
3: oh
1: don't say it

3: my
1: don't say it

3 holds in a thought

2: you didn't say it!
1: I'm honestly impressed
3: it really is—
1 / 2: DON'T SAY IT
CYRANO: [*about the crowd*] look at them, they're gorgeous. thank you so much for coming.

she touches parts of the stage, the set. trots to the edge, down into the audience, looks back

pros arch, huh? we're still doing that? huh. okay

to the audience

I know you're all thinking 'it's too early in the show for this much audience engagement' [*maybe a different voice*] 'oh no, it's a classic, please, leave it alone'. [*maybe a different voice again*] 'god, is it going to be like this the whole time??' [*own voice*] nah, you'll be right…[1]

3 is still staring at CYRANO*'s face*

3: whoa

CYRANO *is on high alert*

CYRANO: who's this?
1 / 2: we don't know
CYRANO: right, well … let's start. are you still a cook in this one?
1: maybe, I haven't decided
CYRANO: look at us, we're hungry. all of us. we're so hungry. can you still be the poet cook, for us?
1: I concede
3: [*still staring*] whoa

CYRANO *pointedly ignores* 3

CYRANO: [*to* 2] and you?
2: I have several carefully delineated characters. I've been working on a limp—
1: and now you're here, we can start
CYRANO: haven't you done that already?

2: we have prepared a small welcome

1 and 2 pull out some party blowers, take a big breath in and—

CYRANO: no, *no.* we do this clean, clear, no sentiment, and no spectacle

1 and 2 drop the blowers into CYRANO's open hand

1: [*with dignity*] it's just an offer
3: [*truly horrified*] WHOA

CYRANO wheels round

CYRANO: hi mate

a tiny pause

something you wanna talk about?
3: no
CYRANO: something about the way I present?
3: nooo
CYRANO: something about me that's different. what is it?
3: nothing
1 / 2: [*sotto*] oooooo
CYRANO: [*with veiled threat*] it's not nothing
3: no, it's not nothing …
1 / 2: oooooo
3: WHAT?
CYRANO: am I not charming enough—is that it?
1 / 2 / 3: nooooooo
1: very charming
2: so charming
3: too charming
CYRANO: too charming?
3: oh god
CYRANO: say it

3 looks at 1 and 2—they shake their heads

say it

3 looks, they shake again

say it
3: it's your nose

a very fraught silence

CYRANO: … what about my nose?

3: [*back against the wall and suddenly spilling out*] it's fucking HUGE

an even more fraught silence

CYRANO: … and?

3: [*can't stop*] christ, no 'and', it's just honestly the biggest nose I've ever seen. it's one of the biggest *things* I've ever seen. it's enormous. I can't take my eyes off it. it's like a car crash on your face. fucking hell

a very tense moment

CYRANO: is this person a friend of yours?

1 / 2: noooooooo

CYRANO: [*to the audience*] yours? [*new thought*] are you a wit? a writer?

3: I do a bit of stand-up

CYRANO: really?

3: open mics

CYRANO: no way

3: but I'm starting to get paid … a bit

CYRANO: paid! paid for your art. paid for your skill. because it's not just a hobby, is it?

3: no

CYRANO: then you can do better

3: what do you mean

CYRANO: the nose. you can do better

3: I don't think I want to

CYRANO: you don't want to? come on, draw your bow, take your aim. you literally can't miss it. are you an improviser?

3: yes. yes, *and* …

a pause

no

CYRANO: you astonish me. just so many angles, so many possibilities. if I were you, I'd start with … one of the classics. 'Cyrano was late, but her nose was on time.' [*invariably the audience will groan*] I didn't say it was good, I just said it was a classic. what about something screamingly modern? 'fuck me, lucky you never got COVID, one sneeze and total annihilation.' something local: 'maaaate, that deserves a statue on a bloody highway: Big Marino, Big Pineapple, Big Nose (actual size)'. horological: 'what time is it? I don't know, get 'er to lie on the ground. it's about (*ten-past whenever the show started*).' while I'm down here, did I ever tell you the one about the dildo farmers? they had a terrible problem with squatters ... agricultural: [*a local farmer's accent*] 'first we had the drought, then we had the mouse plague, then Cyrano stopped and smelt the roses and now we've got nothing left.' televisual: [*Attenborough voice*] 'and here we see the proboscis monkeys have found their new god'[2]

1: are you done?

CYRANO: dunno. [*to* 3] do you want another go?

3 *shakes her head*

then I'm done

3: you act like you're better than everyone

CYRANO: I am better than everyone, and if I didn't look like this, you wouldn't dare fight me on it

2: bitterness is a repellent, you know

CYRANO: [*correcting*] self-awareness is a non-negotiable, though sadly not ubiquitous

1: no one can live on pride alone

CYRANO: no? watch me

3.

1: meet the new girl

ROXANNE *has appeared, and takes in the audience, the space. she prepares herself, a player, ready to join the gang*

2: hang on, didn't they grow up together?

1: not in this version, no. the new girl

2: the old girl

CYRANO: the only girl

1: Roxanne

3: [*singing*] *Roooooxxx—*

1 / 2: no, we're not doing that

CYRANO *rushes to them for information*

2: okay, so. *traditionally*, she's a childhood friend, someone you've grown up with, who knows exactly how wonderful you are

CYRANO: good

1: but who thinks of you only as a friend

CYRANO: less good

1: and she's your cousin

CYRANO: what? no!

1: or, she meets you new, afresh, you don't know anything about her, and she has no preconceptions

CYRANO: that one. yep. that one

2: then you have to deal with her seeing you right now for the very first time. fresh eyes

CYRANO: fuck, no, the other one!

2: too late!

CYRANO *and* ROXANNE *stare at each other.* ROXANNE *smiles, unfazed.* CYRANO *walks towards her, trips*

CYRANO: ha! tripped on a flat stage … this is … ha! wow. this is going well [*to the chorus*] do I get to do it again?

1 / 2 / 3: no

CYRANO: fucksticks

CYRANO *turns to leave*

1: no, look, she's blushing

CYRANO: she's blushing?

1: she liked it

CYRANO: she *liked* it

ROXANNE: I'm not a blusher. I am an unwilling blusher

CYRANO: unwilling blushes are the best kind

ROXANNE: some would say the only kind

CYRANO: that's true. I never go 'oh, I must make a blush now'

ROXANNE *laughs.*

1: laughing, that's good!

CYRANO: a blush is pleasure revealed against better judgement, it's a body's dissent against a logical mind

ROXANNE: pleasure, or embarrassment

CYRANO: … or embarrassment, yes

ROXANNE: it's physical subtext. or maybe all subtext is physical, I mean, it's certainly not verbal

CYRANO: no, true, then it would just be

CYRANO / ROXANNE: text

ROXANNE: Roxanne

CYRANO: Cyrano

ROXANNE: I've heard about you

CYRANO: ah yes, my reputation precedes me … by about six inches

ROXANNE: there's a lot to be said for a well-placed six inches

CYRANO: [*a nervous laugh*] … and you are, what do you (*do*) … ?

ROXANNE: a student. new

CYRANO: what do you study?

ROXANNE: everything. I am voracious. I study the curious alchemy of everyday things. I'm hungry for knowledge, contradictory and complicated. the clear unshakable facts of the natural world. the inescapable misunderstandings of the human heart. the outrageous delight of collective nouns. a loss of umbrellas

CYRANO: an indifference of waiters

ROXANNE: a marvel of unicorns. I study the history of France; how a whole culture, with a thousand unprotectable borders, defined itself as glorious in defeat

CYRANO: *vous parlez français*?

ROXANNE: *absolument*

CYRANO: *définissez, si vous voulez, les principes centraux de l'expression romantique française*

ROXANNE: *philosophique ou poétique?*

1: c'mon, no more of this

CYRANO: what? no! it's part of my heritage. [*gesturing to* 2] he likes it. it's authentic

2: if it were really authentic, you'd be doing it in verse

CYRANO: shall we?

3: no, in English please, and in prose, I'm getting lost …

ROXANNE: the aerodynamics of hummingbirds. the speed with which they cut the air. tiny hearts and lungs all covered in sequins and each one the size of my thumb. the artistry and control required to make the Stone Temple of Petra. the chaos and hope required to turn mouldy bread into penicillin. the genetic ingenuity required to make an Angler Fish. when I am tired, I read the Dictionary of Obscure Sorrows and dwell on *lachesism*—the desire to survive something so cataclysmic it will put a kink in the otherwise smooth arc of my life, and forge me into something greater than I am. how privileged and awful that strange desire is. when I am alight, I read poetry, but of course, doesn't everybody?

CYRANO *is smiling at her*

are you often completely silent?

CYRANO: no

3: really, no

3 *is silenced with a look.* ROXANNE *heads off*

1: so she's everything

CYRANO: everything

2: real manic pixie dreamgirl

ROXANNE: I am not, I'm fully-realised

2: sorry, I didn't know you were still here

ROXANNE: I am very complex

3: [*about* 2] that's what he says too

1: we've yet to see it

2: flaws?

ROXANNE: shallow. as yet unrealised. as yet untested

1: oooo. shall we?

ROXANNE: let's

4.

2: introducing the new boy

CYRANO: what? no! not yet!

YAN *enters, a rock-star entrance, a movie-star entrance, all sex and ease and smoulder, with music and perhaps a wind machine*

[*to audience over the music*] no, c'mon, give me one more scene with her, just one more scene! he gets music?? this is not fair!

YAN *locks eyes with* ROXANNE. CYRANO *is completely invisible to* ROXANNE *now* [*yelling up to the lighting box over the music*] who's lighting this?? I had to do mine in silence and in a wash?? [*to the audience*] no, don't applaud him, you're better than that

music ends. a moment. CYRANO *looks between* ROXANNE *and* YAN

CYRANO: absolutely not. c'mon, they haven't said one word to each other

ROXANNE: who is that man?

CYRANO: yes, good question, who the fuck is he?

ROXANNE: no, really, who is he?

1: oooo, I think it's love!

CYRANO: whose side are you on?

1: we're on the side of *art*

ROXANNE *leaves*

2: [*to* 3] go. do something useful

3: excuse me, hullo

YAN: yeah

3: are you … new? I'm new. too

YAN: I'm a soldier

2: a soldier!

YAN: I think you can tell

YAN *smoulders, or flexes somehow, not necessarily muscles*

1: damn boy

3: I have never

2: I mean, I see it

CYRANO: fucking hell, this is your introduction?

YAN: I'm new and a soldier and I'm interested in the world

CYRANO: are you? in what way?

YAN: I wanna … see bits of it. lots of it. lots of different bits of it

CYRANO *scoffs*

my name is Christian. Yan

CYRANO: Yan? that's how he shortens it? fuck me

YAN: no thanks

CYRANO: no, double no thanks! fuck

YAN: it's blunt. manly / like me

CYRANO: / like him. no, it's interesting. it's *unusual*. you didn't want to go with just good, wholesome Chris?

YAN: Chris is boring. I'm not boring

YAN *does aaaaabsolutely nothing for a moment*

CYRANO: no

YAN: who was that woman?

CYRANO: don't—

1: Roxanne

CYRANO: oh come on

3: [*singing again*] *Rooxxx—*

CYRANO: I wouldn't, mate

YAN: Roxanne, huh? what a babe

CYRANO: nectar from the muse herself

YAN: huh?

CYRANO: nothing

5.

CYRANO: I have exquisite taste. consummate. I can tell, from one sip, which side of a hill a grape was grown on. I can show you the weight of a line in a poem as perfectly as that clod weighs a rock in his hand for throwing. why shouldn't I hunger for the smartest, the kindest, the most vivacious, the most beautiful? why shouldn't my *exceptional* taste extend to the taste my heart has for hope, for joy? why must I be satisfied with the scraps from other people's tables?

a pause

3: because

CYRANO: I KNOW WHY, IT WAS A SOLILOQUY, I WAS SOLILOQUISING

3 *cowers.* CYRANO *changes tack*

do you ever find yourself people-watching? I mean, other than now, obviously. and you see a couple leave a cinema, she turns back to him, smiles with such wattage that you're surprised that he isn't literally pushed back by the power of it, and you're smiling back at her, thinking, my god, if someone smiled like that at me I would stop, I would try to capture that moment, I would hold it in my hands, and here he is, shrugging it off like it's nothing, like it's something to be tolerated on the way to the car, and you think, I could, I could make someone like that smile like that at me, I could, and then you catch your reflection in a shop window and you remember, that's right. that's not for me.

a pause

I forget, sometimes. I honestly … I forget

2: you anticipate pain

CYRANO: I am prepared for it. you can't go in an innocent. that child gets laughed at. that child gets hurt

1: you predict it

3: you / manifest

CYRANO: / don't say manifest

3: I wasn't … I didn't …

2: but you don't want to be loveable, do you? you want to be timeless. incandescent

1: timeless? is this the shopping network? is she a shepherdess figurine?

CYRANO: not loveable like a teddybear

1: like 'worth love'. actually worthy of love

CYRANO *gestures—exactly*

2: I don't know why you're tying yourself into a knot. women don't care about how someone looks

all the women turn on 2

3: don't care?

CYRANO: are women not allowed to be flawed, must we be paragons of virtue

1: this is thinking from the fifties

ROXANNE: I am fully-realised and imperfect and—

1: the 1890s

CYRANO: can women not be sexual?

1: the 1640s

ROXANNE: must we be angels?

CYRANO: empty cyphers?

ROXANNE: pretty little objects for you??

there's more muttering: 'oh, I think I'll faint from all this thinking ...' 'thank you mister big man for telling us what to think.'

2 *is shook*

2: I'm just saying … I'm allowed to have an opinion. my opinion is valuable

1: *is it?*

6.

ROXANNE *sings or dances—she owns the stage. a moment full of life and joy and appetite. glorious. exhilarating.* CYRANO *watches in delight*

this next scene is a meeting of two equals, not a teacher–student dynamic. they are Socratic with each other

CYRANO: denuded
ROXANNE: denuded. it is good. others?
CYRANO: limber
ROXANNE: limmmmber. hoodwink
CYRANO: hoodwink! good word
ROXANNE: great word
CYRANO: and obviously—
ROXANNE: midwifery
CYRANO: yes!
ROXANNE: everybody says midwifery
CYRANO: nobody says midwifery
ROXANNE: no, in the real world nobody
CYRANO: except midwives
ROXANNE: except midwives
CYRANO / ROXANNE: obviously
ROXANNE: but in the 'favourite words' bit of life? it's nothing but midwifery. constantly
CYRANO: huh

new thought

ROXANNE: what's the job of a poet?
CYRANO: the job of a poet?
ROXANNE: is it to make people happy?
CYRANO: ha! no. analysis, maybe? investigation of the world around them? maybe?
ROXANNE: sexy (*it isn't*)
CYRANO: isn't it? (*I know*)

a pause

the job of a poet is to make something more obvious and less obvious at the same time. because you can't just say 'life is short' over and over again—'life is short life is short lifeisshortlifisho'—but you have to make it so inescapably clear in your verse, so that every time someone thinks of 'gathering ye rosebuds while ye may' or 'present mirth having present laughter' or
ROXANNE: or 'time's wingéd chariot / hurrying near'
CYRANO: / hurrying near' you all beat with the same heartbeat, just for a moment. life is short. life is short
ROXANNE: this is what love feels like. this is what love feels like

CYRANO *hears this*

[*a little challenge, a game*] how would you describe … (*me?*)
CYRANO: well, I wouldn't insult you by comparing you to a summer's day
ROXANNE: I wish you wouldn't
CYRANO: but I would … make me a willow cabin at your gate
ROXANNE: I would halloo your name to the reverberate hills
CYRANO: doesn't count, same / speech
ROXANNE: / but it's later!
CYRANO: it's the same speech and it does not count
ROXANNE: hmmmm. I would, wait … let me count the ways
CYRANO: I want to do with you what spring does with cherry trees
ROXANNE: this is what love feels like this is what love feels like
CYRANO: life is short life is short
ROXANNE: you're not alone you're not alone you're not alone
CYRANO: … yeah
ROXANNE: you know, love is the only thing that requires eternal optimism
CYRANO: that sounds tiring

ROXANNE: it is. but think about it. let's say … falling in love is a job. in any other occupation, if you kept being knocked back, you'd take the note, you'd change your profession. but love is the only thing where you have to go in, again, for the first time, every time. not bring your pain, and your trauma and your despair. you have to go in an innocent

CYRANO: innocent

ROXANNE: hoping against hope, every time

CYRANO: yes

ROXANNE: I've been thinking … about someone … a lot

CYRANO: oh?

ROXANNE: we only met the other day, but I could feel it already

CYRANO: oh

ROXANNE: it was instant

CYRANO: instant

ROXANNE: and now I can't stop thinking about them

CYRANO: oh

ROXANNE: I know, I know, it's insane. and of course, they were silent

CYRANO: I know, stupid, wasn't it!

ROXANNE: yes!

CYRANO: I mean, you have that effect on people

ROXANNE *dismisses this*

ROXANNE: it's not someone I would usually fall for

CYRANO: no

ROXANNE: but life is made for risk and adventure

CYRANO: it is

ROXANNE: I need to get a message to them

CYRANO: please, allow me to … pass your message on

ROXANNE: really? thank you

CYRANO: and what shall I tell … them

ROXANNE: tell them to make a move

CYRANO: oh

ROXANNE: I want them

CYRANO: oh my god

ROXANNE: tell them, they take my breath away

CYRANO: oh!

ROXANNE: tell them to say something to me, finally!

CYRANO: ah—what?

ROXANNE: they haven't said one word to me

CYRANO: I mean some words, maybe not the best words

ROXANNE: not one. it's madness. tell them they're so handsome

CYRANO: …

ROXANNE: so handsome, I can barely remember my own name around them

silence from CYRANO

Christian. Yan. he's new

more silence

CYRANO: … yes

ROXANNE: I knew you'd know. right? I mean, even you can see

CYRANO: *even* I can, yeah

ROXANNE: he's so …

CYRANO: … butch

ROXANNE: [*with delight*] yes!

CYRANO: but you … you won't be, you couldn't be satisfied with … Roxanne, what if he's dumb as a bag of hair

ROXANNE: no, he has the eyes of a poet

CYRANO: ha

ROXANNE: or, not a poet, but his eyes brood and glower, like a movie star

CYRANO: famously smart, movie stars

ROXANNE: what?

CYRANO: nothing

ROXANNE: all that brawn with all that brain inside. I know it. one without the other would be untenable, but together, irresistible

CYRANO *hears this*

I think he's shy. tell him to talk to me. I know that brain is exploding with bliss notes, and dopamine, and white-water rapids of logic and euphoria

CYRANO: you know this

ROXANNE: I know this. he can't just be beautiful, it wouldn't be right

CYRANO: no

ROXANNE: it wouldn't be fair

CYRANO: no

ROXANNE: so you'll talk to him? tell him?

CYRANO: … of course. anything (*for you*) … to be useful

ROXANNE: acts of service

CYRANO: that's the one

ROXANNE *starts to leave, delighted.* CYRANO *thinks she's alone*

I want to break something

ROXANNE: what?

CYRANO: nothing, sorry, just … do you ever have that feeling where you want to crush something? rampage?

ROXANNE: why?

CYRANO: no reason, a desire to feel your power.

3 *makes a tiny noise somehow*

you

3 *squeaks*

come here

ROXANNE: no

CYRANO: I can't stand idiots

ROXANNE: don't hurt—

CYRANO: I won't … I just … come here

3 *approaches as if to the guillotine*

she's a fool. she won't feel it

3: won't feel what?

CYRANO: see?

ROXANNE: you'll eviscerate her

CYRANO: good word

ROXANNE: your temper, Cyrano

CYRANO: the world is made for people who don't look like me

ROXANNE: there's violence in you

CYRANO: you don't know. you don't know what it's like to have to fight, all the time

ROXANNE: … don't I?

ROXANNE *leaves*

a dreadful pause. CYRANO *is mortified*

1 *breathes in to speak, and—*

CYRANO: I heard it, I heard it, as soon as I said it, I heard it. fuck

another pause

CYRANO *retreats to the edge of the playing space*

2: well that was awkward

the chorus is on eggshells

a pause

1: do you want something to eat?
CYRANO: I'm not hungry
3: [*quietly, after a little pause*] … I am actually starving
1: come on. I'll make you a snack and a metaphor. go on. it'll be nourishing.
2: 'nourishing'
1: that attitude—
2: sorry
3: what will your metaphor be?
1: I don't know. so many to choose from … oysters

possibly, 1 *produces an oven from the stage and begins to bake/cook throughout this next scene, possibly not …*

2: oysters?
1: how oysters were the poorest food, and lobsters too, when you look at them you see why, they're prehistoric and they cling to sea walls, and you have to narrowly avoid slitting a vein to open them, and they're filled with silt and muck
3: I thought they were fancy
1: exactly! over generations they became the finest food, the most desirable, served on white tablecloths with simpering staff and the kind of wine with just a blank space where the price should be
2: god, I love those places. all that pomp and folderol. the hats!
3: hats?
1: and then they
3: do we get hats?
1 / 2: no
1: what I'm saying is … there's something to be said for scraps

all look to CYRANO

CYRANO: next

1: alright. what about … recipes

3: don't you just read them in books?

2: [*to* 1] you should. too much improvisation in your cooking. why not just stick with the classics

1: because you can't just repeat and repeat, even the act of repeating changes the product, the act of a different person doing the 'same' thing makes it different. ask a thousand different roti makers, all across India, and you'd get a thousand different roti recipes. front of the fire, back of the fire, how long you knead, how long you prove, what part of your hand you mix with, and this is a *two-ingredient* bread

3: and everybody's favourite is their mother's. my mum makes the most amazing—

1: but you don't learn how to cook by blindly following a recipe. you learn, by fucking up: that cream needs lemon juice, salted pig *needs* sour tamarind, how those perfect balances ping the appetite—you *need* depth of flavour and complexity. sugar needs to *nearly burn* to make a caramel. things, appetites, *art* shouldn't be simple. it's not satisfying like that. you learn, by fucking up, how you save a dish from disaster and plate a triumph

CYRANO: next

1: it's just an offer

CYRANO: well make it a better one

2: yes, none of these have been your best

1: [*losing patience*] listen. food is mess. life is mess. you don't cook a perfect meal, offer it up all fringed by rosemary and glistening with artisanal peppercorns, to look at it and never touch it. this business of living is *designed* to dribble down your chin and ruin your expensive linen napkins

CYRANO: so what's your metaphor, a perfect thing destroyed is beautiful?

1: it's only the amateur cook that mourns the loss of the perfect artifice. the professional leans forward, eyes alight, as the knife plunges in

CYRANO: are you calling me an amateur?

1: professional writer, amateur human being

this lands. a moment

3: [*proud*] it's what's on the inside that counts

everybody turns and stares at 3

with the meal—the metaphor … isn't it? I thought that's what you were (*going for*) …

2: [*gesturing to the audience*] they're not paying for that

3: what?

2: they're not paying seventy-five dollars a ticket for 'it's what's on the inside that counts'. I'm not having it[3]

3 *drops her head*

1 *produces a piece of cake from somwhere, and proffers it to* CYRANO

CYRANO: I told you I'm not hungry

1: it's not for you. this (*theatre*) isn't for you

1 *gestures to the crowd*

CYRANO: [*looking up*] sorry. sorry

CYRANO *gives the piece of cake to the front row*

[*to the audience*] sorry

2: oi. too many metaphors, not enough plot. now. how are you going to compete with that wall of meat?

1: he's beloved by everybody

2: you don't even have any friends. anyone to recommend you

CYRANO: aren't you my friends?

1: god, no. we're the chorus. changeable, us

2: I have several distinct characters

1: are you ever going to show us any of them?

3: do we have a bad guy, in this one?

2 *starts to preen*

2: De Guiche!

3: who's that

2: the bad guy. in the original. he's a duke, or a viscount. or something. I don't know, it's French

1: if you can't remember why the original is better, why do you keep bringing it up?

2: the past is just better. than this. I'm just saying

CYRANO: I think all the bad guys are in my head

1: ah. modern

2 *deflates*

3: you can be a bad guy for me, if you want

2: for you? I don't wanna be a bad guy for you, I wanna be a bad guy for Cyrano. the play's called 'Cyrano'. I don't wanna be the mortal enemy of Chorus Member Number Three. there's no nobility in that

CYRANO: is there nobility in evil?

2: oh yes. stand by what you believe, even if it hurts others. a drivenness, a singlemindedness. the desire to achieve. evil is epic. big and huge and impressive. can't miss it. gotta be wowed by it, even if you don't … you know, enjoy it. same with sadness. it's very … uniting. I can say [*to the audience*] 'you know sadness' 'you know loneliness and longing' and I know everybody does. and has. and will again. inevitable. you know where you stand with pain when you're a Greek chorus. and then there are portents, and keening, and beseeching—

1: we're a French chorus

2: a French chorus is a can-can. I call on Ye Gods, I beat my chest, slaughter deer and pour libations, and it still doesn't work, the ending's still the same. it's terrific

1: effective

2: what?

1: nothing

2 *gathers his dignity*

2: I'm just saying, there are all sorts of ways to get what you want

3: [*wise, helping*] you can't make an envelope without breaking eggs

a very long pause. everybody turns and looks at 3

CYRANO: …what?

3: you can't … make an envelope … without … it's a saying

CYRANO: who says it?

3: … lots of people

a tense moment

CYRANO *advances on* 3. *stops herself*

CYRANO: what's your name
3: me?
CYRANO: yes you. what's your name
3: … um …

3 *thinks for as long as the audience can stand it*

CYRANO: forget it

CYRANO *loses patience and leaves*

1: you didn't have a name ready?
2: you have to have your character name ready, you only get one chance to be a named character
3: I didn't … am I a *named character*?
1: not anymore
2: sorry buddy, you snooze, you lose

7

ROXANNE: ah. the handsome boy
YAN: ah, the … hi
ROXANNE: hello
YAN: … hey
ROXANNE: what an evening. don't you love these nights, when the air is still and hot, and you know the breeze is coming, but it isn't here yet. the air is oppressive, yes, but thick with possibility
YAN: yeah
ROXANNE: and those first little whips of the wind, those invisible fingers, impish, getting up under skirts, inside jackets, making little dogs crazy
YAN: yeah. I love dogs
ROXANNE: do you?
YAN: … yes. especially. little dogs
ROXANNE: ah

ROXANNE *waits a moment, bemused, then leaves*

8.

CYRANO *sits.* YAN *joins. there is weird silence for a bit.* YAN *produces a beer. one for* CYRANO *too.* CYRANO *accepts. they crack them, and* YAN *clinks* CYRANO*'s bottle. they drink*

YAN: … women, huh?
CYRANO: … mmm
YAN: that one, for instance. am I right?
CYRANO: are you?
YAN: she's so … / chatty
CYRANO: / brilliant?
YAN: she's not responding, though. not responding like usual. to the classics. you had me at hello. you complete me
CYRANO: classics is such a strong word
YAN: I have great qualities
CYRANO: uhuh
YAN: just not chat, y'know?
CYRANO: I'm getting that
YAN: I need a good line. to open with. hey. you like lines
CYRANO: I like words, there's a difference
YAN: is there? I don't get what the big deal is. with words
CYRANO: you don't see the appeal of words?
YAN: no
CYRANO: all words, or are there ones in particular you don't like?
YAN: nah, it's just … bodies, I get. bodies make sense
3: your body particularly
CYRANO: [*to* 3] are you right, sweetheart?
YAN: [*deep*] like … why … writer
CYRANO: why … what?
YAN: what's a writer's worth? be a soldier. make an impact, you know. maim a guy
2: PLEASE
YAN: a soldier would … just take her, right? don't worry babe, I've got this, climb a tower, throw her over a shoulder, here's your happily ever after

CYRANO: I could be a soldier, you don't know
2: yeah, but you haven't fought, so
CYRANO: [*suddenly huge, swift and physically terrifying*] I will fight you in a fucking instant mate, do you want that?
2: no, actually, no, no I … good point, no

a little pause

[*quietly*] you can be very emasculating
CYRANO: can I? good

YAN *applauds*

YAN: okay, so, look, man to man
CYRANO: … okay
YAN: I should just be cool, right? be … direct. Roxanne, I love you
CYRANO: you don't know her
YAN: I know what I know. I love her. I love her I love her

YAN *starts spinning*

CYRANO: Yan. Yan. if you say that to someone you don't know, you're a stalker
YAN: fuck. I thought it was romantic. nah, you're right. whoa, I'm dizzy

YAN *sits down suddenly*

I'm gonna talk to her. I'm gonna—I'll write a speech
CYRANO: will you? how will you begin this speech
YAN: Roxanne, I love you
CYRANO: we're going in a loop here
YAN: nah, nah, I should lead up to that. got it. I don't want to startle her, so she runs. like a wild animal. [*a little noise of discovery*] metaphor
CYRANO: [*echoing that noise*] simile. and I think you should avoid language that makes her skittish and fearful and the feeling that you need to trap her. I don't think that plays well
YAN: mmm. mmm. mmm. I've got to make it seem like it was her idea
CYRANO: so close. it's got to be her idea, she has her own (*ideas*). look, you can't just tell her what she is, what she's thinking, your words lead her to a thought, but she makes the link, let *her* wit, crisp and clear as champagne and just as intoxicating—

YAN *gets a little notebook and pen from somewhere*

YAN: hang on, I'm writing this down

CYRANO: your words should be something that makes her lighter, buoyant, like

YAN: helium

CYRANO: … yep, or … they should be something that … fill her, like

YAN: spakfilla. *expandable* spakfilla[4]

there is a silence

CYRANO: … yep

YAN *writes*

but don't … don't write that …

CYRANO *carefully takes the notepad from him*

look, all your words are foreplay, every word you say to her from here on in is foreplay, each poem—

YAN: oh god, *poems*

CYRANO: no, ah … each poem contains the key to its own lock

YAN: that doesn't sound very safe

CYRANO: no, not (*literally*) … a word, or a phrase unlocks the code, and different phrases unlock different codes for different people

YAN: that's not how locks work

CYRANO: …

YAN: somebody needs to explain a bunch of things to you about locksmiths. locksmithing

3: locksmithery

YAN: that

CYRANO: you think writing has locked you out. you hate words because you think *they think* they're too good for you. but they're not. they're … ginger and yuzu and duck fat, they're nothing until they're combined and transformed. you don't hate words, Yan. you're jealous of how impenetrable a perfect sentence is, so you've never tried. and until you've tried, until you grind curry paste from scratch, until you make cumin pop in a pan, you will always be jealous. of a *take-away*

1: now she's on board with the cooking metaphors.

everyone looks at 1

I'm just saying, she wasn't before, but now she is

CYRANO: yes, now they're useful to me

YAN: you write so nice. you talk so nice

CYRANO: 'so nice'

YAN: ah, don't be a fuck about it. I've seen the way you look at her. I've seen you

CYRANO is silent

you can't speak your truth

CYRANO: that's … pseudo-psycho-babble

YAN: I know you can't. you're a coward

CYRANO: I'm no fucking coward

YAN: speak it through me. you could seduce her. you could. under the … [*trying something*] cape of my flesh

they both deal with exactly how disgusting that image is

a pause. they look at each other. they look away

CYRANO: if I could borrow your body

YAN: if I could borrow your mind

they look at each other

CYRANO: fuck you

YAN: fuck you

they look away again

CYRANO: if …

YAN: together we could …

CYRANO: shhh

a moment

I could make you perfect. my words in your body

YAN: we could

CYRANO: *we* could be perfect

YAN / CYRANO: together

CYRANO: the perfect lover. the soul of a woman in the body of a Greek god

YAN: I'm from (*wherever the actor is from*)

everybody deals with this

the soul of a woman in the body of a (*wherever the actor is from*) god

turns to go again, then turns back

no, you're right. yours was better

a tiny moment

see? I'm getting it

YAN *leaves*

3: what are you doing
1: this isn't what you want
2: you should kill him
CYRANO: what??
2: just kill him instead
1: you want her to deal with a grieving woman? howling with tears?? it would never work
CYRANO: yes, *that's* the reason I shouldn't do that
3: but this isn't what you want, right?
CYRANO: who is this?
1 / 2: no idea

CYRANO *moves downstage*

9.

music. CYRANO *looks out to the crowd, not at what she creates*

CYRANO: you want to know why words, Yan? you want to see the power of words? here I write 'her balcony appears' and so it appears

a balcony rises up out of the stage, ROXANNE *atop it. the chorus rush to hang festoons from it.* YAN *watches, transfixed*

trails of sparkling globes, Roxanne's cheekbone catches the light. you see it, don't you?
YAN: [*astonished, watching*] I do, I see it
CYRANO: that's the power of the written word. that's why you become a writer.

CYRANO *gathers herself*

alright. go on
YAN: [*top-of-his-voice yelling*] ROXANNE

CYRANO: gently, gently, man, c'mon
YAN: [*whispered*] Roxanne
CYRANO: but still heard

CYRANO *takes over for a second*

Roxanne
YAN: oooo, you are good

YAN *motions to* CYRANO *that he can do this first bit by himself*

finally. we are … alone
ROXANNE: yes
YAN: the night is ours
ROXANNE: … yes
YAN: all alone

ROXANNE *is silent*

ROXANNE: … yep

ROXANNE *takes a different tack*

do you remember being a child, Yan?
YAN: um, yeah. but I'm … not a child. right now. don't worry
ROXANNE: do you know they don't have truffle pigs anymore?
YAN: is this connected to me being a kid? or—?
ROXANNE: the pigs are too hungry, too ready to gorge themselves, they scarf down the truffles before their handlers can get to them. I always thought, when I was a kid, I'm going to be the kind of grown-up who's a danger to truffles. I'm going to run at every invite, take fistfuls of every dessert, ride on the back of Vespas with strange men. throw parties dripping with streamers and paper hats and surprisingly heartfelt karaoke. I'm not going to be the kind of person who says, 'oh, those dates are a bit difficult, yeah, but with the traffic, oh, a nightbus? no, no, I don't think so'.[5] I'm going to be a truffle pig. I will truffle for pleasure. I'll be exhausted and fat and poor and it's going to be fucking wonderful
YAN: I'm going up
CYRANO / 1 / 2 / 3. NO
ROXANNE: we can't
YAN: but
ROXANNE: we mustn't

YAN: you literally just said
ROXANNE: no
YAN: what? why?
2: it's a balcony scene Yan, there are rules to this shit

YAN *stops*

ROXANNE: but to imagine, and not do? agony. *I love it*
YAN: but … truffles …
ROXANNE: talk to me. talk sweet to me. talk nasty to me

CYRANO *goes to help, but is shooed away again*

YAN: Roxanne, I … I want you
ROXANNE: yes.

a pause

and?
YAN: and? I want you
ROXANNE: and …
YAN: and … I want to … do everything to you. on you
ROXANNE: everything? what?
YAN: I want to … touch your tits
1 / 2 / 3 / CYRANO: [*sotto*] oooo
ROXANNE: do you think I value myself so low I would give this body away?
YAN: dinner first?
1 / 2 / 3 / CYRANO: [*sotto*] oooo
ROXANNE: I want to hear my value in your words
YAN: I want to *value* your body
1 / 2 / 3 / CYRANO: [*less sotto*] oooo
ROXANNE: goodnight

CYRANO *starts feeding* YAN *lines*

CYRANO: I don't speak when you're around because I worry language will be insufficient
YAN: I don't speak when you're around because I worry language will be insufficient
ROXANNE: …
CYRANO: that my feelings will force me into cliché. Hallmark cards
YAN: that my feelings will force me into cliché. Hallmark cards

ROXANNE: the death of romance

CYRANO: I don't want to embarrass you with platitudes

YAN: I don't want to embarrass you with platypus

EVERYBODY: hmm? / what's that? / sorry?

CYRANO *takes over, becomes* YAN*'s voice*

CYRANO: I don't want to embarrass you with platitudes

ROXANNE: ah. please don't. or with platypus. where would I keep them? what do they eat?

CYRANO: but who ever thought words would not be enough?

ROXANNE: cliché is … what's the opposite of a panty-dropper?

CYRANO: a leg-crosser

ROXANNE: a cement knicker

CYRANO *laughs.* YAN *looks disgusted*

YAN: that's fucken weird, man

CYRANO: to be here now, the courage it takes to be here now, talking to you like this, I have to imagine myself as the man you want, not the worthless thing that I am. I've cast this movie in my head, and it's not me playing me, but it is me, the way it is in dreams

ROXANNE: what are you?

CYRANO: unworthy

ROXANNE: you put me on a pedestal. I am human. your words make me untouchable

CYRANO: you are untouchable

ROXANNE: I am flesh and fury. I am mistakes and repair and work

CYRANO: work? are you a fabrication? a lie?

ROXANNE: a life's work. years of making choices, easy and hard, years of sticking to them, years of changing my mind, of unlearning things. forgiving myself. examining my motives. work

CYRANO: that's good work

ROXANNE: could you love a fabrication? a lie?

CYRANO: that's a loaded question

ROXANNE: is it?

CYRANO: I … I would want to know why someone was lying

ROXANNE: a lie is a lie

CYRANO: a lie to protect someone beloved from the horrors of the world

ROXANNE: is misleading

CYRANO: is misleading
ROXANNE: but understandable
CYRANO: but understandable!
YAN: nothing about this is understandable
ROXANNE: why don't you come creeping through the streets to find me? I want you to come creeping through the streets to find me
CYRANO: leap over a railing
ROXANNE: yes
CYRANO: scale a wall
ROXANNE: yes yes
CYRANO: maybe I have, maybe I'm there right now
ROXANNE: in front of me
CYRANO: out of breath
ROXANNE: the rush of desire surprised you
CYRANO: it does
ROXANNE: but you came
CYRANO: I did
ROXANNE: you came for me
YAN: I could
CYRANO / 1 / 2 / 3: no
ROXANNE: then …
CYRANO: then … a kiss
ROXANNE: no
CYRANO / YAN: no??
ROXANNE: it's not about the kiss
CYRANO: I don't (*understand*) …
ROXANNE: it's about the moment before the kiss. how you read each other's bodies before you touch. when you breathe the same air for a second. I love that. I love that the most. the breath in your ear, the breath on your face, pure fucking pheromones. the stuff that makes the poetry make sense—the reason there are so many love songs

CYRANO *laughs again*

that was a funny laugh, who did that sound like, someone
CYRANO: noooo …
ROXANNE: that sounds like someone's laugh, who is it

CYRANO: [*back on track*] so, the moment before the kiss, when I first risk touching you, first put a hand at your waist, and …

ROXANNE: the air changes

CYRANO: yes. the air changes. everything charged, the molecules around your mouth electric. I can feel the kiss before it's begun

ROXANNE: yes yes

YAN: and now …

CYRANO: and now …

ROXANNE / 1 / 2 / 3: and now?

CYRANO: not yet

everybody wriggles in delicious frustration. YAN *in frustration not quite so delicious*

YAN: what? why not?

CYRANO: sit

YAN: more than sit. get her to do more than sit

CYRANO: sit

ROXANNE *sits. it is exquisite*

hands on the bed beside you

ROXANNE *does it*

there. the curve of your jaw where it meets your neck, the feeling of the back of your skull resting perfectly in my palm, I know how, when I kiss you there, my breath on your ear, hot, ragged, when I twist my hand in your hair, I know how your skin prickles all over, how you rise up to meet me, your body working before your mind can stop you

ROXANNE: why would my mind stop me

CYRANO: no reason

ROXANNE: you've imagined this

CYRANO: a thousand times. a hundred thousand times

ROXANNE: and you're not tired of me? you haven't shrugged me off to find some other fictional lover

CYRANO: I can't be tired of you

ROXANNE: oh, it's not the same each time, this fantasy?

CYRANO: different at every second, at every turn. sometimes the infinitesimal movements of sharing a bed, friendly, but neither asleep, a slight adjustment met with the slightest of push backs, sometimes a hand against the wall above your head, a lean, my best Jimmy Dean, let's get the hell outta Dodge, baby, just you and me

ROXANNE: are you sad you only get one beginning?

CYRANO: I am furious that time is linear, to only get one beginning with you. I want a thousand. I want a hundred thousand. sometimes you break up with me

ROXANNE: I break up with you? why?

CYRANO: sometimes you hate me

ROXANNE: I couldn't

CYRANO: you could. I've had every conversation with you

ROXANNE: every one, except an actual one

CYRANO: … yes

ROXANNE: every experience except an actual experience

CYRANO: … yes

ROXANNE: you've cut me out of the narrative

CYRANO / YAN: no

ROXANNE: yes. this is just you, ventriloquising. you in female form

CYRANO: is that so repulsive?

YAN: oi

ROXANNE: you could have any form

CYRANO: any form?

YAN: oi

ROXANNE: I could desire any form that contained that mind

CYRANO: Roxanne, I need to—

YAN: OI

1 / 2 / 3: shhhhh!

ROXANNE: [*a perfect pivot*] the mind that has anticipated my every move, my every thought, that has dictated my every response, that has left me no room for my own input

CYRANO / YAN: … noooo …

ROXANNE: are you frightened of what will happen?

CYRANO: yes

YAN: oi

ROXANNE: scared of what might be

CYRANO: yes

YAN: oi

ROXANNE: scared of how good it could be
CYRANO: yes
YAN: OI
ROXANNE: so you keep me in your fantasy
CYRANO: I do
ROXANNE: selfish
CYRANO: smart
ROXANNE: you keep pleasure from me
CYRANO: yes, and pain. and disappointment
ROXANNE: why would I be disappointed?
CYRANO / YAN: no reason …

YAN *drags* CYRANO *away*

CYRANO: Yan, mate, go home, this is not about you
YAN: don't fuck me around
ROXANNE: christ, I want you
CYRANO / YAN: ohhhhhh
ROXANNE: god, I wanna fuck you
CYRANO / YAN: fuuuuuuuuuuuck
YAN: I'm going up
CYRANO / 1 / 2 / 3: you can't
YAN: she wants me
CYRANO: she doesn't want you
YAN: she's imagining me
CYRANO: she's fucking herself with my words
YAN: your words with my body
CYRANO: you try doing your body without my words, and see where that gets you
ROXANNE: why are you silent? was I too bold?
CYRANO / YAN: no
YAN: I will come for you. I will fuck you
CYRANO: there's that poetry
ROXANNE: yesss

YAN *looks to* CYRANO*—he's winning*

YAN: I will fuck you … hard
ROXANNE: [*less certain*]… yes

YAN: and … a lot
ROXANNE: ah, I was too filthy. I have a sailor's mouth. this is—(*not what I want*)

CYRANO *takes over again*

CYRANO: no. I'm glad there's salt in that mouth
ROXANNE / YAN: salt?
CYRANO: yes, because if you were just relentless sweetness …
ROXANNE / YAN / 1 / 2 / 3: what?
CYRANO: … I wouldn't be so hungry for you
ROXANNE / 1 / 2 / 3: yesssss
YAN: alright, maybe you're winning now
CYRANO: oooo, I think I am
YAN: but when I can touch her, I'll be winning then, fuck your words
CYRANO: fuck your words, the guy's a wordsmith
YAN: SHUT UP
ROXANNE: why are you silent?
CYRANO / YAN: *no reason*
YAN: DON'T SHUT UP, KEEP TALKING
ROXANNE: I need you to come for me
CYRANO: I can't … I can't do that, Roxanne
ROXANNE: I need you to come to me, I need you
CYRANO: / I can't, I can't do that, please, Roxanne, I can't
ROXANNE: / I need you, I need you, I need you

YAN *pushes past* CYRANO, *scales the balcony and kisses* ROXANNE. *music. a* YAN *and* ROXANNE *love scene.* CYRANO *is under the balcony, echoing just the barest of physical gestures of what's going on above. incredibly hot, but also, agonising and impossible. their three-way love affair*

10.

in a twist, ROXANNE *and* CYRANO *are huddling together as only two dear female friends can*

CYRANO: so. how was it?

ROXANNE *thinks*

ROXANNE: like fucking the statue of David

CYRANO: ha! well, I'm not going to make a small dick joke here, because we're better than that

ROXANNE: we are. and he is. it's huge

CYRANO: of course it is. it was a classical antiquity thing, the small dicks, the fig leaves. it was about the mind's control over the body

ROXANNE: imagine having control over such a perfect body

CYRANO: … imagine. so, come on, tell me everything, I must know every detail …

ROXANNE: it was … prosaic

CYRANO: ??

ROXANNE: plodding

CYRANO: plodding. PLODDING. he would be devastated to hear that, I'm just going to very quickly tell him…

CYRANO *goes to leave*

ROXANNE: [*squealing*] stop! come back here!

CYRANO: she commands it, I return

they huddle together again

ROXANNE: I mean … it was good. honestly. acrobatic. relentless

CYRANO: relentless!

ROXANNE: I mean … there's probably a better word than relentless, a word more suited to passion. inexhaustible, maybe?

CYRANO: insatiable?

ROXANNE: yeah, maybe… but I do mean relentless. as it went on, it got more … Olympic. I am personally impressed by how flexible I am. I came. a lot

CYRANO: that's great

ROXANNE: but … to love a person's language, and not be able to communicate when they're in the room. it's a problem. it's like he's two totally different people

CYRANO: … men

ROXANNE: do you think that's it? that they're so conditioned not to talk about their feelings that he can only do it … when he's not looking at me? when I can't see him?

CYRANO: I think that's probably it

ROXANNE: I suppose I have to encourage him. reward good behaviour

CYRANO: it's like training a dog

ROXANNE: really, though, the fire went out of me. I had to go into the bathroom and read his messages to get going again

CYRANO *breathes*

CYRANO: Rox—

ROXANNE: why can't it just feel like it does when I'm with you?

CYRANO: ah …

ROXANNE: easy, and bubbling along, slaloming down black diamond slopes

CYRANO: well … because

ROXANNE: of course

CYRANO: … of course

ROXANNE: but you … with a dick

CYRANO: classical antiquity dick or big-dick-energy dick?

ROXANNE: somewhere in between, like—

ROXANNE *measures out the nose on* CYRANO*'s face, like—exactly this size! it's a joke, but is completely mortifying to* CYRANO. *the atmosphere turns, sharply*

I'm sorry. I wasn't—

CYRANO: no, it's fine. it's fine, don't worry

ROXANNE: oh god, I'm so sorry

CYRANO: no, it's fine. really. it's fine.

a tiny pause

that's what it's there for. jokes

an awful pause

so, me with a dick. I mean … I could just nip out to Kings Cross, get ya something[6]

ROXANNE: [*glad to be let off the hook*] you know what I mean

CYRANO: I know what you mean

ROXANNE: but to look like that and be so shy! it's madness! what is he frightened of?

CYRANO: the woman needs verse, flow, poetry. note taken

ROXANNE: notes for who?

CYRANO: no one

ROXANNE: you must have a beau

CYRANO: a beau?? [*Southern, perhaps a mimed fan*] 'will I take them down to the summerhouse for a barbecue? my word, but the heat can just make a girl wilt this time of year' I'm in a corset, obviously. 'oh my… a beau? who, for lil' ol' me? a beau!'

ROXANNE: c'mon! you've got to be interested in someone …

CYRANO: ah …

ROXANNE: you are, look at you

CYRANO: I am … interested in someone

ROXANNE: who?

CYRANO: you wouldn't believe me

ROXANNE: who??

CYRANO: she is a … an astronaut

ROXANNE: really? wow!

CYRANO: yep, wow. she's exploring Mars at the moment. not on Mars. obviously. that's not a thing. you would have heard about that. she's just … near Mars

ROXANNE: where is she now?

CYRANO: … how much do you know about the night sky?

ROXANNE: nada

CYRANO: that's so lucky

CYRANO *points out constellations—has to get close to* ROXANNE *to do it*

well, you see, um … you see Orion's Belt, there, the three stars … then she's just, um … she's just … there … [7]

ROXANNE: so, you wouldn't see her much

CYRANO: no, we find other ways to communicate

ROXANNE: you'd be good at that

CYRANO: I am

ROXANNE: what's she like?

CYRANO: … breathtaking

ROXANNE: breathtaking! you've never described me as breathtaking

CYRANO: have I not?

ROXANNE: no

CYRANO: what, are you jealous?

ROXANNE: ha! no …

ROXANNE *starts to move away*

CYRANO: wait … *are* you jealous?

ROXANNE: no

CYRANO: Rox—

YAN *enters, and* ROXANNE *runs to him*

ROXANNE: here he is, this big, beautiful, throbbing, dripping

YAN: [*delighted*] steady on

ROXANNE: MIND of a guy! ooooooft. honestly, look at you. this is all so good [*his body*] ugh—

she rubs herself up against him

but this mind, fuck! I really think I could fancy *anyone* with this mind. you could look like anything, and I'd be like … UGH GOD YES TALK TO ME SAY THOSE WORDS

there's a pause as everybody deals with this. ROXANNE *backs up from* YAN*'s chest*

and here we are again. silence

YAN: yeah, I …

CYRANO: Roxanne

ROXANNE: … are you upset? why?

CYRANO: Roxanne

ROXANNE: you've got to know, right, I was obviously joking. *obviously* I find you devastatingly attractive. obviously

CYRANO / YAN: … obviously

ROXANNE: sorry, Cyrano, were you saying something?

ROXANNE *turns to face* CYRANO *with a dazzling smile.* CYRANO *is silent.* YAN *looks at her*

CYRANO: me? no

11.

CYRANO: I don't want to fight, Yan. I'm tired. let's not Solomon this baby. take her. make her happy

YAN: I'm not winning on a *forfeit*. that's pathetic. I'm not pathetic

CYRANO: can't you just be happy you won?

YAN: she doesn't want me

CYRANO: she does

YAN: she wants you

CYRANO: she doesn't want me, she doesn't even think of me, I am nothing to her

YAN: *I'm* nothing to her. did you hear her? I could be anybody. you could recast me mid-scene and she wouldn't even notice. like, I could be Chris Hemsworth, or Chris Evans or Chris Pine or Chris Pratt, but like, now, not fat like before, and she wouldn't even notice the difference. [*a big thought*] sometimes I wonder how much I'm plot and how much I'm punchline

CYRANO: … you wonder that?

YAN: yeah. I mean, not all the time. mostly I'm aware I'm a pretty central figure

CYRANO: okay

YAN: hero. love interest. save the city, come with me, get to the chopper. but this … something's off. something … I don't feel right. OH MY GOD, I'm fat Pratt

CYRANO: what?

YAN: I am fat. Pratt

CYRANO: you're not fat Pratt

YAN: I am, I'm on that show with that intense blonde lady in all the hallways, I'm fat Pratt, I'm fucking comic relief. this hurts. I … *hurt*. [*locking eyes with* 2] you. you wanted pain, you wanted suffering, now look at me. I'll kill you!

YAN *lunges at* 2—CYRANO, 1, *and* 3 *restrain him*

CYRANO: Yan, mate, calm down, you're having some sort of psychotic break

3 *is helping by stroking* YAN*'s body*

2: oh god
1: you wanted unravelling. *this* is Greek
2: not from him! not from the soldier. I don't want the soldier to have a breakdown. this doesn't happen in real life
1: I think it does
2: well, not to this extent and I don't like it
CYRANO: are you okay, mate?

YAN is breathing heavily

YAN: I'm a bit … I think
1: you're hyperventilating, you need to—
3: you need to put your head between my knees

YAN does this. everyone watches, deeply bemused

a moment

YAN brings his head up

YAN: thanks. I feel better

3 glows

a pause. a shift

CYRANO: why do we keep telling the old stories?
YAN: huh?
CYRANO: they're such old stories
YAN: because they're good
CYRANO: they're sad, Yan. they're so sad
YAN: what?
CYRANO: they end badly. for everyone
YAN: I don't know, they usually work out alright for me
CYRANO: even for you. in the old story. you go off to war. all of you. you don't come back
2: [*his greatest praise*] it's brilliant
CYRANO: I just … I wouldn't mind a happy ending, now and then

a pause

YAN: [*sniggers*] happy ending

3 and YAN laugh

CYRANO glares at them both and leaves

2: we'll have a rebellion on our hands soon, and then what

1: then what?

2: exactly. then what

1: no, I mean … what happens in a rebellion? in a revolution?

2: well, the Old World falls, the old order, then unrest for a while, and then … people live their lives, I suppose. but there's no time, no time to fight, no time to wrestle the narrative away from … from where it always goes. no time to do it again, just stick in your lane, head down, and try and get through it, that's the way, barrel on through to the end

1: … why rush to the end if it's a tragedy?

a long pause

2: I'd learn to dance, you know. if I could do it differently. if I had the time to … do it again. I'd dance

1: really? what kind of dancing?

2: well, something

he looks about … cautiously gets up

something like …

2 *dances. it is, perhaps, popping and locking*

2 *sits, a bit flushed*

something like that, but … professional, you know. professionally

a little silence

1: I like your dancing

2: really? well. thanks …

a moment

2: do you wanna see some more?

1 *nods.* 2 *dances for her. then* 1 *gets up and joins him. everybody dances for a while.* ROXANNE *tries to draw* CYRANO *into the dance. the chorus try too.* CYRANO *keeps herself separate.* ROXANNE *dances with* YAN

12.

CYRANO: I could live like this

3: what?

CYRANO: I could live like this. with a fragment of her. the last flash of her smile. just to know she looks for me, in a crowded room, when she makes a joke. it's enough

3: what? no!

CYRANO: it is. if it has to be

2: it does

CYRANO: I could live with her stolen mid-afternoons and her late-night afterthoughts

2: look at her bend so she doesn't break

CYRANO: I could live with the drunken calls when she tells me her day, and asks me to help her sort it into filing cabinets in her head

2: look at that *compromise*

CYRANO: I can do it

2: the sacrifice

3: and never touch her?

2: the veiled despair

1: never be held by her?

3: you deserve better than this

CYRANO: nobody deserves anything. this is what I am *allowed.* my allowance of love, my allowance of dignity, my daily allotment of sunshine and fresh air and her laugh. just enough to live on. I can do it

3: you can't. this can't be a tragedy. we've got so much tragedy

CYRANO: is it a tragedy to survive?

3: like this, yes

2: look at that resignation! magnificent

3: you have to ask for more

CYRANO: and risk losing my daily ration? I can't, I need this to live

1: you could have a feast

2: a feast, or lose everything and starve. that's the gamble

1: it's not fair to her

CYRANO: she'll never know

1: how do you know

CYRANO: [*near tears and thick with fury*] because I'm better than everybody … because I'm good at this

2: you're good at everything

CYRANO: [*with despair*] yes

3: [*quietly*] well, not everything

CYRANO: I'll do it because I can. I'll hold it so she doesn't have to

13.

a very quick lighting change and CYRANO *is completely together. a total tonal shift—domestic and easy. they are perhaps making tea*[8]

ROXANNE: I propose a treatise on the body

CYRANO: a treatise on the body? words on the invisible violence of limbs

ROXANNE: good

CYRANO: is it? I think it's overwritten. anyway. go on

ROXANNE: one. that small skirmishes, risks and roughness as a child, mean you can throw a punch when you're grown, that you know how to grab your bag and run quickly, scale a wire fence, it's not a complete surprise to your body the first time violence happens as an adult. I was attacked once, I crumpled like a paper bag, I crumpled like a *cliché*, I didn't even put my hands up, I didn't know how, my body didn't know how, and all the times I'd scoffed at how women collapsed in movies—'why don't you run'—it's because I wasn't inoculated by pain as a child

CYRANO: … good word. so, what, pain is necessary

ROXANNE: for growth?

CYRANO: maybe just … pain is necessary

ROXANNE: kinky

CYRANO: ... if you say so

ROXANNE: two. have you ever been stretching

CYRANO: stretching

ROXANNE: stretching, very specifically your neck, and you think oh yes, just a fraction further, a millimetre, a tiny increment, you breathe out and you realise that one night you might be so relaxed that you just … snap your own neck

CYRANO: …

ROXANNE: and for a second, you'd be holding your own broken body in your hands, before your nervous system caught up and dropped you, and you would have a moment of awake-ness where you realised what you'd done, like those heads that stay alive after the guillotine, blinking, and in that moment, that one, final moment, you also realise you have inadvertently created the greatest murder mystery of all time

CYRANO: this is not where I thought any of this was going

ROXANNE: three. do you ever wish you were in somebody else's body?

CYRANO *chokes on her tea*

CYRANO: do I ever … it's crossed my mind, once or twice, why do you ask?

ROXANNE: I just … sometimes I wonder, if I didn't look like this, I'd know

CYRANO: know what

ROXANNE: exactly, empirically, how smart I am. sometimes I think men are so astonished by the fact that I can string a sentence together, and they're so desperate to sleep with me, that they laugh at all my jokes and say 'you're, like, so fucken smart'[9] but they're not actually thinking about what I'm saying. if I didn't look like this, I'd know. I'd have rigorous, scientific testing. about exactly, empirically how smart I am. [*new thought*] and how funny

CYRANO: you're smart

ROXANNE: yeah?

CYRANO: and funny

ROXANNE: and deeply fuckable

CYRANO *laughs*

CYRANO: there's that salt

ROXANNE *turns very slowly*

ROXANNE: … what did you say?

CYRANO: what did I say, I said 'there's that sa—'

CYRANO *catches herself. they stare at each other*

ROXANNE: I didn't tell you about the salt

CYRANO: … yeah, you did

ROXANNE: I didn't. I remember every single one of our conversations

1: [*very, very quiet, almost inaudible*] no

ROXANNE: I didn't tell you

CYRANO: ah, maybe…

2: [*almost inaudible, dark and quiet*] this is it, *this* is why you're so unlovable

3: now hang on

ROXANNE: did he?

CYRANO: no

ROXANNE: *did he?*

CYRANO: he didn't, it's not, he didn't—

1: [*so quiet*] she'll be destroyed

2: [*so quiet*] can't be trusted, fetid, wrong

ROXANNE: that laugh

CYRANO: no

1: [*quiet*] she'll never trust anyone ever again

ROXANNE: I recognise that laugh

CYRANO: no. I—

2: [*slightly less quiet*] foul from the inside out

ROXANNE: say my name

CYRANO: what?

ROXANNE: say my name

3: [*slightly less quiet*] no, don't do it

ROXANNE: gently, not whispered. still heard

CYRANO: [*from the balcony scene*] Roxanne

ROXANNE *breathes in*

ROXANNE: you

1: [*slightly less quiet*] you've ruined her

CYRANO: listen, I—

1: [*a little more audible*] the one thing you loved

ROXANNE: YOU

CYRANO: I

ROXANNE: every word? every wor—?? oh my god

ROXANNE *removes herself*

1: very, *very* bad

2: it's not your face. it's you. you're broken

3: I don't think this is helpful

2: 'oooo, I don't think this is helpful' she's just lost the only chance she'll ever have at happiness and you're all, like: 'ooo, I read the back of a self-help book once.' this is TRAGIC. this is epic and very big and sad and now people are going to suffer. *finally*

14.

ROXANNE: so my job is to remain beautiful and untouched. fuck you. fuck that. I'm better than that

CYRANO: you are

ROXANNE: you made a child of me. you made my decision for me. don't trouble your pretty little head about it, does baby want an ice cream?

CYRANO: that's true

ROXANNE: you made me an ornament. some exotic fruit. a prize[10]

CYRANO: you're right

ROXANNE: *stop agreeing with me*

CYRANO: I do agree with you

ROXANNE: and yet. *your actions*

CYRANO: you wanted him, his perfect body, his movie-star eyes. your shallowness is showing

ROXANNE: your catfishing duplicity is showing

CYRANO: yep, that's fair

ROXANNE: also, I'm allowed to be shallow, I'm fully-realised

CYRANO: yeah, I insisted you be

ROXANNE: *fuck you.* is this how you get your kicks?

CYRANO: no

ROXANNE: no. this isn't how you get anything. you made me the last person to know something. *me.* you made them [*the audience*] laugh at me

CYRANO: [*quiet*] they weren't laughing at you—

ROXANNE: speak up

CYRANO: they weren't laughing at you—they're on your side. I think. they're not on mine

ROXANNE: I wonder why. are you meant to be the hero of this? [*to the chorus*] is she?

2: well, traditionally—
ROXANNE: FUCK TRADITION
1: I mean, not a hero-hero, but a
CYRANO: [*muttered*] tragic hero
ROXANNE: what?
CYRANO 1 / 2 / 3: [*slightly more audible, but only just*] tragic hero
ROXANNE: can you have been a hero now and have done all this? all of you? you stood by and watched. you *cheered.* whose side are you on?
3: [*helping*] we're on the side of art
1 / 2: [*gritted teeth*] not now
ROXANNE: you're as bad as the old ones
CYRANO: what?
ROXANNE: the old white guys who used to tell this story, you're exactly the same. say it
CYRANO: what?
ROXANNE: 'what?' say what you did. namc it
CYRANO: wh—
ROXANNE: c'mon, use your big girl words, say it
CYRANO: I lied
ROXANNE: and
CYRANO: I manipulated you
ROXANNE: and
CYRANO: and what, I ruined you, spoiled you
ROXANNE: do you think that's it? I don't mind having slept with him, have you seen him? look at him. really, look at him. that is a notch any belt would be proud to have
CYRANO: I'm glad you had a good time
ROXANNE: so am I, otherwise this gets real grim real quick
CYRANO: I didn't want you to have to decide against me. I wanted to spare you the shame of being loved by this, by me
ROXANNE: and what if I didn't?
CYRANO: what?
ROXANNE: what if I didn't decide against you?
CYRANO: … what if you didn't?
ROXANNE: you're afraid of that
CYRANO: no … yes … what?

ROXANNE: you think you're so fucking smart. you fucking *Frankenstein*

CYRANO: that's not why … this wasn't an experiment

ROXANNE: wasn't it? but it's why you thought you could get away with it. stand back, separate, *safe*, and dandle us all like little marionettes. because you're so fucking clever. betrayal. the *betrayal*

CYRANO: the betrayal is on both sides

ROXANNE: … *what??*

CYRANO: betrayal of your principles. 'oh, Cyrano why can't it feel like it does when I'm with you', 'I could desire *any form* that held that mind'

ROXANNE: I—

CYRANO: and the betrayal of my own body. this thing, this *thing* that can never satisfy you. never satisfy anyone. that I'm enough to be your best friend, lift you up, hold you, shelter you from the horrors of the world, but I'm not enough to love. I'm not good enough to love

a pause. CYRANO *sits*

ROXANNE: if I were a young woman and you were an old man

CYRANO: this would be bad, this would be very bad, I see that

ROXANNE: so what is this?

CYRANO: … romantic comedy?

ROXANNE: I'm not laughing

CYRANO: no

a moment

ROXANNE: how do we get out of this

CYRANO: I don't know. it's a metaphor

ROXANNE: what

CYRANO: this whole thing, it's a metaph—

ROXANNE: it's my life. this is my *life*. I used to blossom in sunlight, fill up a room. congratulations. you made me small. and you made me stupid

ROXANNE *leaves. there is silence for a long time*

3: … what happens in the original?

CYRANO: I'm dying, so she has to forgive me

2: and now?

CYRANO: well, we're all dying, just some of us more acutely than others

a pause

3: but … what now? don't stop, you can't just stop

CYRANO: now, nothingness

3: what?

CYRANO: now, the empty page

CYRANO *starts pulling apart the set*

3: no

CYRANO: run a flag up the mast in the middle of my face, I surrender

2: bit fatalistic, but sure

CYRANO: fuck scenes, fuck other people, I'm better alone. go on, I'll do you an encore of all those funny little speeches about my great big problem, then we can all call it quits. you think I was done before?? I hadn't even started. I've got hundreds more. 'Mount Rushmore called, it wants its mountain back' 'and it's gold gold gold for Australia with a near perfect six-point-nine from the Russian judges, using her own nose as the balance beam'

1: but—

CYRANO: clear the decks, everybody out

she storms down into the audience

1: you can't just—

slams open an auditorium door

CYRANO: get out

3: but

CYRANO: GET OUT GET OUT GET OUT

1 *and* 2 *shuffle sheepishly toward the exit*

3: [*quiet, terrified, but doing it anyway*] … no

1: what?

3: … no

everybody looks

[*still frightened, but braving it out*] … the self-pity. honestly. you're embarrassing yourself

CYRANO: you don't understand, you couldn't possibly und—

3: don't I? you think you're so special, but *everybody* feels this. everybody feels a version of this. that this wonderful person could never love me, because 'reasons'

2: because 'reasons'

1: go on

3: we're all telling ourselves we're not worth it because, well, actually, I don't know why, maybe we feel safer, or maybe [*important*] it's magazines, but really, it's all in our head. whatever it is. like … I'm not that dumb. and you're not *that* ugly. but you think you are and that's exhausting. but you've got such brio, such flare, so much panache and such a big, big heart, honestly, I barely even notice the … y'know

silence as 1, 2 *and* 3 *await the tirade*

CYRANO: [*quietly*] good word, panache

3: [*thrilled*] is it? [*recovering*] yeah. no. it is. I thought so too. look. you can bring this back

CYRANO: I can't

3: you can! you can add vinegar and truffles and Ovaltine and we can all nom nom nom on a big plate of triumph[11]

2: that the most disgusting thing I've (*ever heard*) —

3: [*a bit wild*] you were all so pleased with your cooking metaphors, and now I'm doing one and you can just shush up! [*back to* CYRANO] you can turn this around

2: there's no guarantee that she can

3: that's part of it … I think

1: not knowing?

2: better to know, safer to know

1: she can't talk her way out of this

2: talking's what got her into it

3: no more talking!

1: something … bigger than words

2: [*scoffing*] bigger than words?

1: a gesture

3: a big one

2: we can help!

CYRANO: I don't need help. I don't need anybody's help

a tiny pause

I need help

chorus rush to CYRANO. CYRANO, 1 *and* 2 *leave the stage.* 3 *is left alone*

there's a pause

3 *starts singing the first line of 'Roxanne' by The Police*

this isn't going well, but still 3 *persists, singing the next couple of lines*

YAN *appears, joining in with* 3

YAN: I've been wanting to do that since we began
3: right??

they smile at each other. sit in comfortable silence. YAN *takes a breath to speak, and—*

no more poetry, please. it's draining
YAN: isn't it?

a pause

YAN: those guys are kind of mean
3: yeah, well, not mean, just … they don't have any idea what it's like to be us
YAN: what's that?
3: [*very deep*] not them
YAN: [*equally deep*] totally

a pause

3: I … I like you
YAN: I like you

a pause. they look at each other. look away. look back. they kiss! then smile at each other

3: there
YAN: right?
3: no need to overcomplicate it
YAN: totally. I'm Christian. Yan. Chris. what's your name?

a momentous pause

3: Charlotte

blackout

15.

music.[12] *everyone bustles about transforming the space. someone puts on a party hat and hands them out to others—there are hats for the audience too. ask the audience to pass streamers, hats, and festoons along—we need their help!*

ROXANNE *appears on the balcony, or in the auditorium*

CYRANO *takes a big breath and ... sings*

she sings for a bit but ... it doesn't work. ROXANNE *turns to go. it isn't enough*

CYRANO *fights tears. the chorus come to her rescue and join the song. more people singing is ... slightly more persuasive.* ROXANNE *allows it*

the chorus unroll a large banner saying 'she's very *sorry'. a second banner—'she fucked up'*

ROXANNE *is watching now.* CYRANO *tries again, sings another verse*

CYRANO *dances. it's not very good. it has bits of* 2*'s and* ROXANNE*'s dance in it, perhaps bits of everybody's dance in it.* ROXANNE *smiles*

slow lights up on the crowd. CYRANO *sings to them too*

ROXANNE *is coming around. she sees the crowd, sees the beautiful chaos of the stage.* CYRANO *starts to hope. more light on the crowd now. the gentlest of confetti falls over the stage. delicate, beautiful, messy. and everyone's in it. maybe encourage the audience to join the song*

ROXANNE *joins the stage picture. music moves to underscore*

ROXANNE: did you write this bit?

CYRANO: I don't know. I honestly … I don't know. we made it for you. we all of us … made it for you. but … you don't have to like it, you don't have to be a part of it. it's just …

ROXANNE: … no fixing these old stories

CYRANO: … no
ROXANNE: creaky old plots
CYRANO: … yes. no. no
ROXANNE: nice offer, though
CYRANO: thanks

chorus and CYRANO *turn to go, conceding defeat. all is lost*

ROXANNE: I'll do something new with you

CYRANO *turns*

… if you want

CYRANO *nods, barely, doesn't want to break the spell*

CYRANO: start again, start clean, start bare
ROXANNE: start silly. start messy. here. all this chaos
CYRANO / ROXANNE: uncontrollable
CYRANO: yes
ROXANNE: … good. and now, instead of perfect impossible fictions, you get

ROXANNE *lifts some confetti, streamers, mess from the ground, sprinkles it over* CYRANO. *she takes* CYRANO*'s hand and puts it at her waist*

CYRANO *doesn't know what to do*

would you describe yourself as courageous?
CYRANO: [*still not quite holding her, babbling, stuttering*] I would—I do—generally—I think people would—
ROXANNE: but not now
CYRANO: not *now*, no, not now

CYRANO *breathes.* CYRANO *takes her up into her arms. they're face to face. the moment before the kiss*

the air changes

16.

under a very, very slow lights out, CYRANO *and* ROXANNE *sit in the mess of the stage, confetti falling all over them, all over the audience now too, perhaps tiny pieces of ripped-up script*

ROXANNE: I want to take you to every restaurant in the city, every single one, and we'll say to the waiters 'just bring us what you think the best food is, no don't tell us, just bring it to us'

CYRANO: I want to take you to a museum in Amsterdam and kiss your neck amongst the Rembrandts, the marble that looks like flesh, how did they do that

ROXANNE: let me bring you things I found on my walk, a little blue eggshell

CYRANO: this rock with a sad face on it

ROXANNE: this perfect leaf, bright red from the tree

CYRANO: let's go to a cabin in the woods together

ROXANNE: can it be a log cabin?

CYRANO: it *has* to be a log cabin

ROXANNE: let's get very rich and own a log cabin

CYRANO: let's own several and give them away to friends

ROXANNE: let's never get rich, let's always work and know the worth of our work

CYRANO: yes, let's get our hands dirty and sleep well at night

ROXANNE: do you snore?

CYRANO: I don't know. do you snore?

ROXANNE: we'll find out. let's have a garden

CYRANO: yes, let's have a garden, with a big old table out the back and we'll throw a sheet over it, and serve up lamb we cooked for hours

ROXANNE: I'm vegetarian

CYRANO: and serve up eggplant we cooked for hours

ROXANNE: let's invite lots of people over

CYRANO: they'll drink wine and laugh

ROXANNE: and none of them will leave

CYRANO: and at three a.m. we'll reluctantly call some of them cabs

ROXANNE: and the rest of them we'll wedge about the house

CYRANO: a sofa here

ROXANNE: a window seat there

CYRANO: a little corner of the kids' room, sweep the lego out of the way with a foot and roll them in covered in coats because we've run out of blankets

ROXANNE: … kids!

CYRANO: how many do you want

ROXANNE: how many am I allowed

CYRANO: send me a photo of the little lemon cake you had for afternoon tea

ROXANNE: the one with the sugar crust

CYRANO: that we bought from the lady in the market with the sharp black bob

ROXANNE: send me a photo of your eyes in that meeting

CYRANO: 'Janine is doing another one of her wacky presentations'. can you explain algebra to me?

ROXANNE: a bit. can you explain NFTs to me?

CYRANO: a bit. let's see bad comedy in a back room in the East Village

ROXANNE: let's get lost in a Turkish spice market and come out with our skin dry-rubbed with clove and cinnamon

CYRANO: let's drink watery mojitos in Cuba on days so hot we can't sit down

ROXANNE: the seats will scald the back of our legs

CYRANO: then let's get headaches from the day drinking and have to go to bed in the middle of the afternoon and listen to the world pootling on outside our window

ROXANNE: car horns, shouts of people, a hammer drill, the smell of someone pressing waffle cones, gasoline, jasmine. an enthusiasm of five-year-olds

CYRANO: a massacre of parking fines

ROXANNE: an exaltation of larks

CYRANO *and* ROXANNE *kiss and the lights fade*

the end

ENDNOTES

1 Cyrano is essentially doing crowd work here. your job, Actor-Playing-Cyrano, is to get the audience to love you, to get them on your side. pull out every charm offensive that you have. three good jokes in the first minute should do it. I've included some of the material we used, but it I also changed it every day. so, make it your own—this moment is a kind of bridge, a liminal space between you and Cyrano, so it works well if they're your own jokes

2 again, make this your own, friends. local jokes, current material. tailor to your audience, and the world around you. go for it!

3 I'm sure it's clear that this should be whatever ticket price you're charging, but just in case it isn't …

4 in the UK this is Polyfilla, in Australia this is Spakfilla, and if there are any more regional variations, this is my note to honour them

5 again, get specific with this, tailor this to your locality, and to your Roxanne. reference whatever current transport nightmare there is—bridges, roadworks—or, if Roxanne is tall, the length of the flight and her long legs, etc, etc

6 local and specific here, my loves! You can go a famous brand, or your local area known for sex shops

7 use your own patch of sky here, reference the stars that you and the audience are under …

8 if you wanna do the shorter version of this play, we have a super quick way into this scene which I've included in the additional materials

9 use whatever language here feels right for this Roxanne and this Yan. Roxanne might be able to directly quote Yan, or mimic his voice, or you might wanna use language that gets used towards women on the streets where you live. again, make it personal, make it your own

10 these words were gifted to me by our awesome UK Roxanne Jess Whitehurst, when she was talking about ways that she has been made to feel in various spaces. if there are words that are more

specific to your Roxanne, and to her lived experience, use them. but please always end with 'a prize'

11 go local, loves! something that would be disgusting in combination with those other things, but something deeply, deeply local. We've had Milo, Horlicks, Ovaltine (in the exclusively malted milk department), but what other local stalwart can you reference? what makes (non)sense for your 3 to call on here?

12 the song we used was 'Open Arms' by Elbow, and we loved it. you might find something else to use, or you might write your own. important themes are mess, fuss, community, apology. something that requires the audience to do something, to apologise for being complicit in the way this unfolded, is super useful as well. we got them to wear hats and to throw streamers (on the lyric 'a volley of streamers') to be a part of the lo-fi magic of theatre, and to be a vital part of making the final image so different from the first …

ADDITIONAL MATERIALS

I dearly hope that you are never faced with a global plague that closes theatres and requires people never to gather. but if you are, or if, for any reason, you've have been closed or quiet or away from live performance, you might like to use this opening. this was how our Melbourne season started, directly out of massive lockdowns

PRELUDE

very little light

an empty stage

the cast look at the audience

CYRANO: look at them out there
ROXANNE: heaving
YAN: spitting
1: sweating
3: lactating
ROXANNE: all up on each other
CYRANO: did you see the queue for the bathrooms?
2: did you feel the crush in the foyer as everybody battled to get their little sandwich?
3: on top of each other
1: elbowed her out of the way
ROXANNE: braying with laughter
YAN: I saw this guy crash-tackle his mate to the floor.

a pause

it was awesome
CYRANO: masc

ROXANNE *laughs*

1: everybody's so close
2: close is right, you can smell 'em

CYRANO: right up in each other's grill, under each other's skin, rubbing each other the wrong way, every which way, pressing, shoving, agitating the human soup

a pause

wonderful, isn't it?

blackout

SHORTENED SCENE 13

this is our quick way into scene 13, if you're doing a shortened version of the play, as we did for Edinburgh

13.

a very quick lighting change and CYRANO *is completely together. a total tonal shift—domestic and easy*

CYRANO: tea?

ROXANNE: of course

CYRANO: of course. two sugars and so much milk?

ROXANNE: of course

CYRANO: so, a hot wet milkshake

ROXANNE: it's not your best

CYRANO: sorry

CYRANO *turns away*

ROXANNE: hey. you're distracted. you're thinking about something

CYRANO: am I? what am I thinking about?

ROXANNE: [*putting her hand up to* CYRANO *to read her mind*] dirty bitch

CYRANO: sprung

CYRANO *hands* ROXANNE *her tea. they sip*

ROXANNE: do you ever wish you were in somebody else's body?

CYRANO *chokes*

CYRANO: do I … it's crossed my mind, once or twice. why?